Community Helpers

Veterinarians

by Dee Ready

Reading Consultant:
Dr. Sheldon Rubin
American Veterinary Medical Association
Public Relations Council

Bridgestone Books
an Imprint of Capstone Press

Bridgestone Books are published by Capstone Press
818 North Willow Street, Mankato, Minnesota 56001
Copyright © 1997 by Capstone Press
Printed in the United States of America

Library of Congress Cataloging-in-Publication Data
Ready, Dee.
   Veterinarians/by Dee Ready.
   p. cm.--(Community helpers)
   Includes bibliographical references (p. 24) and index.
   Summary: Explains the clothing, tools, schooling, and work of veterinarians.
   ISBN 1-56065-514-3
   1. Veterinarian Medicine--Juvenile literature. 2. Veterinary Medicine--Vocational
guidance--Juvenile literature. [1. Veterinarians. 2. Veterinary Medicine. 3. Occupations.]
   I. Title. II. Series: Community helpers (Mankato, Minn.)
SF756.R43 1997
636.089'06952--dc21

                                96-47312
                                   CIP
                                   AC

Photo credits
Faith Uridel, cover
FPG/James Levin, 4; Jonathan Meyers, 6; Stephen Simpson, 8; USDA, 10;
  Jerry Driendl, 12
Unicorn/Alon Reninger, 14
James Rowan, 18
Michelle Mero Riedel, 16, 20

Table of Contents

Veterinarians

Veterinarians are animal doctors. They are also called vets. Vets care for sick animals. They help healthy animals stay that way.

What Veterinarians Do

Veterinarians try to make sick animals better. Sometimes vets must operate to help a sick animal. They also set broken bones. Vets sometimes give shots to animals.

Different Kinds of Veterinarians

There are different kinds of veterinarians for different animals. About half of all vets take care of pets. Other vets help farm animals and horses. Some vets work at the zoo.

What Veterinarians Wear

Veterinarians who work in an office usually wear lab coats. Vets who work on a farm wear tall, rubber boots and coveralls. A coverall is a one-piece suit worn over clothes to keep them clean.

Tools Veterinarians Use

Veterinarians use the same type of tools as human doctors. But a vet's tools are made just for animals. Vets use a stethoscope to listen to an animal's heartbeat. They use a syringe to give shots.

Veterinarians and School

Veterinarians must have at least two years of college. Then they go to veterinarian school. Vet school lasts for four years. After they finish school, students must pass a state exam to be vets.

Where Veterinarians Work

Most veterinarians work at animal hospitals. Animal hospitals have examining rooms and operating rooms. There are also places for sick pets to stay. Farm vets go to the home of the sick animal.

People Who Help Veterinarians

Veterinarians need help with their work. A receptionist answers calls for office visits. An assistant helps the vet operate. Often the pet owner or farmer helps the vet, too.

Veterinarians Help Others

Veterinarians help both animals and people. They take care of people's pets. Sometimes they help farm animals have babies. They show people how to care for their animals.

Hands On: Care for Birds

A veterinarian's job is to care for animals. You can care for animals that come to your own backyard.

Birds are everywhere. They need people to care for them. Here are some ways you can care for the birds.

1. Leave birdseed out on your porch or window. This will keep your birds fed.
2. Make a birdbath. Birds like to clean themselves in a bath. Leave some clean water in a pie plate for them.
3. Get a birdhouse. You can buy a birdhouse at a store. Or you can build one of your own. A birdhouse gives the birds a safe place to live.

Words to Know

community (kuh-MEW-nuh-tee)—a group of people living in the same area

examine (eg-ZAM-uhn)—to look over closely

lab coat (LAHB KOHT)—a long cotton coat that covers the clothing

operate (AHP-uh-rate)—to cut open a body to fix a medical problem

stethoscope (STETH-uh-skope)—a medical tool used to listen to the sounds of the chest

syringe (suh-RINJ)—a tube with a plunger and a hollow needle used to give shots

Read More

Gibbons, Gail. *Say Woof! The Day of a Country Veterinarian.* New York: Macmillan Publishing, 1992.

Goldreich, Esther. *What Can She Be? A Veterinarian.* New York: Lothrop, Lee & Shepard, 1972.

Kuklin, Susan. *Taking My Cat to the Vet.* New York: Bradbury, 1988.

Sobol, Harriet Langsam. *Pet Doctor.* New York: G. P. Putnam's Sons, 1988.

Internet Sites

James Herriot Page http://www.wpi.edu/~mazz/herriot.html
VetNet http://www.vet.net/

Index